D1505687

IT'S AMAZING!
SUPERCARS

Annabel Savery

A+
Smart Apple Media

Published by Smart Apple Media, an imprint of Black Rabbit Books
P.O. Box 3263, Mankato, Minnesota 56002
www.blackrabbitbooks.com

Printed in the United States of America at Corporate Graphics,
North Mankato, Minnesota.

Published by arrangement with the Watts Publishing Group LTD, London.

Library of Congress Cataloging-in-Publication Data
Savery, Annabel.
Supercars / Annabel Savery.
p. cm.—(It's amazing!)
Includes index.
ISBN 978-1-59920-691-2 (library binding)
1. Sports cars—Juvenile literature. 2. Automobiles, Racing—Juvenile literature. I. Title.
TL236.S295 2013
629.222'1—dc23
                    2011026533

Planning and production by Discovery Books Limited
Managing editor: Laura Durman
Editor: Annabel Savery
Designer: Ian Winton

Picture credits: Corbis: p. 5 (Transtock), p. 11 (Bruce Benedict / Transtock), p. 16
(Transtock), p. 24 (Bruce Benedict / Transtock), p. 25 top (Transtock); Getty Images:
p. 22 (Hugo Philpott/Stringer), p. 23 top (Fiona McLeod/Contributor); Jaguar:
p. 21; Koenisegg: p. 10 (carstudio.it), p. 14 (Stuart Collins); Lamborghini: p. 15 top;
Rex Features: p. 27 (Sony Pics/Everett), p. 28 (Everett Collection), p. 29 top (Erik C
Pendzich); Shutterstock: title & p. 8 (Olga Besnard), p. 4 (Neil Roy Johnson), p. 7 top
& p.7 bottom (Maksim Tooome), p. 9 & p. 31 (Max Earey), p. 15 bottom (Max Earey),
p. 17 (Max Earey), p. 18 (DDCoral), p. 19 (Dongliu), p. 20 (Tito Wong), p. 23 bottom
(Jaggat), p. 25 bottom (Anatoliy Meshkov), p. 26 (KSPhotography), p. 29 bottom
(breezeart.us); www.carphoto.co.uk: p. 6, p. 12, p. 13.
 Cover: Corbis (Guy Spangenberg/Transtock)

PO1434 / 2-2012

9 8 7 6 5 4 3 2 1

CONTENTS

All words in **bold** appear in the glossary on page 30.

SUPERCOOL SUPERCARS!

Supercars are the fastest, most expensive cars on the road.

They are made to be light and sleek, like this Ferrari. They have huge engines so that they can travel fast.

Supercars are really rare. They are expensive to build and buy, so car companies do not make many. For example, McLaren only made six copies of their supercar, the F1 LM model.

Street Legal

Even though supercars can go incredibly fast, they are still made for people to drive on the roads. Racing cars, like those made for NASCAR, are not street legal. They can only be driven on the racetrack.

THE DESIGN

Supercars are not designed to carry lots of people or a load of groceries. Every part is designed to make them go fast and look great!

Gull wing doors

Lots of supercars have **gull wing** or scissor doors. This means they open upward, instead of outward. On some cars the roof lifts up too!

Supercars are built so that they are very close to the ground. This means that only a little bit of air can pass underneath them. They also have a very **streamlined** shape so that air travels over them easily. Both of these **features** help the car to go faster.

IT'S AMAZING!

The Maserati MC12 supercar lifts up at the front so that it can go over speed bumps.

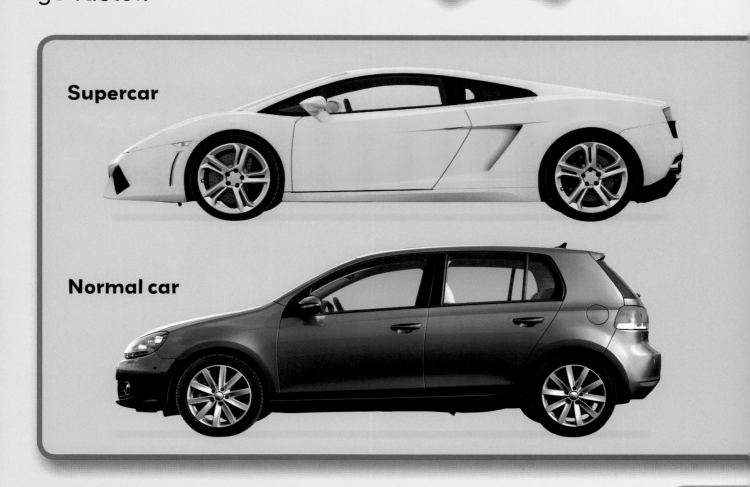

Supercar

Normal car

KEY FEATURES

Every part of a supercar has a special function. Look at the labels to find out what each part is for.

Spoiler This helps to keep the back end of the car on the ground when traveling at high speeds.

Body This is made from a very light material, such as **carbon fiber** or **aluminum.** This means that the engine does not have to carry too much weight.

Engine The engine is very powerful. A supercar's engine may be in the middle, not in the front like most cars.

Brakes The brakes are made of a special material to help the supercar brake quickly at a high speed without getting too hot.

Did You Know?
A car engine's power is measured in horse power (hp). The average normal car has between 100–200 hp. Supercar engines often have more than 600 hp!

TOP SPEEDS

So, how fast is fast? A normal car's top speed would probably be less than 110 miles per hour (177 km per hour).

Supercars are much faster. Some can travel at speeds faster than 250 mph (400 kph).

One of the best things about supercars is their **acceleration**. They can reach high speeds much more quickly than normal cars.

NOW THAT'S FAST!

The Bugatti Veyron (above) can reach 60 mph (96 kph) in 2.5 seconds. An average car might take between 8 and 10 seconds to reach that speed!

MAKING A SUPERCAR

Supercars give designers the chance to see how high-tech they can make a car.

Not many supercars are built, so they are often made one at a time. Each part is designed and crafted to be the best it can possibly be.

The picture above was taken in the Bugatti factory. Each Bugatti Veyron is put together by just eight people!

People who buy supercars can decide what they want them to look like. Buyers can choose the color of the inside and outside of the car, and can ask for any special **gadgets** (see page 15) that they want inside it.

One of a Kind

British businessman Peter Saywell wanted a Pagani Zonda Cinque, but all five had sold out. So, he commissioned Pagani to make one just for him. Here it is!

BEHIND THE WHEEL

The inside of a supercar is just as highly designed as the outside.

Supercars must have everything that a normal car has. A shifter, steering wheel, dials to show the speed, a **fuel gauge**, and so on. But in a supercar they are much cooler.

GREAT GADGETS!

Supercars are often filled with fantastic gadgets. The Lamborghini Gallardo LP 570-4 Superleggera has a rear view camera under the back spoiler!

Newer supercars often have screens inside that allow drivers to switch from regular street mode to racing mode with a simple touch.

ON THE RACETRACK

As speed limits on the roads are the same for every car, supercars cannot travel any faster on roads than other cars.

If supercar drivers want to test out their high-powered engines, they have to go to a racetrack. Here, drivers can compete for the fastest lap times.

On the racetrack, there are long, straight sections where the cars can go as fast as possible.

IT'S AMAZING!

In racetrack tests, the Lamborghini Reventón (above) reached an average top speed of 210 mph (340 kph)!

AUTO SHOWS

Each year, at different locations around the world, large, glamorous auto shows are held. These are the most important days of the year for car designers.

At auto shows, car designers show off their latest supercars. Car **manufacturers** want to impress the visitors with the latest technology.

Many of the supercars shown at auto shows are **prototypes** like the Ferrari below. These are the first models that are made from the designs.

Inspirational Cars

Auto shows are like big car fashion shows. Other car makers are inspired by the top prototype designs. They use these ideas to make simpler versions that become the regular cars that everyone can buy.

ELECTRIC SUPERCARS

One of the biggest problems with cars is that they are very environmentally unfriendly. Their engines produce **exhaust fumes** that pollute the air.

GREEDY SUPERCARS!

Supercars have huge engines that need a lot of fuel to run. Some only travel 4 miles on a gallon of gas (1.7 km/L)! Normal cars travel around 30 miles per gallon (11.25 km/L).

Exhaust pipes

Car manufacturers are working on designs to make cars better for the environment. **Hybrid** cars have been developed that run on both liquid fuel, such as gas or diesel, and electricity.

Electric supercars look just as cool as other supercars, and they travel just as fast. One of the top electric supercars is the Jaguar CX75 (above).

SUPERCAR OWNERS

Supercars cost lots of money, so not many people can afford to own them. They are usually bought by people who are very rich. Some even own more than one!

Car Collection

Jay Kay of pop group Jamiroquai has a big car collection. Among them are a black Ferrari Enzo and a red Lamborghini Miurathe supercar (below).

Supermodel Jodie Kidd (right) loves cars. She owned a Lamborghini Murcielago (right) and now has a Lamborghini Evolutioné. Her other favorites are the Bugatti Veyron and the Maserati MC12.

Lewis Hamilton

Race car driver Lewis Hamilton has been promised a unique McLaren F1 LM supercar if he wins two Formula 1 championships!

SOME OF THE BEST

The Bugatti Veyron, McLaren F1, and Ferrari Enzo are fantastic supercars.

The Bugatti Veyron (above) is the most expensive supercar. It costs $1,700,000, and that's a basic model! It is also the fastest supercar. In tests it has reached 267 mph (429 kph).

The McLaren F1 LM (below) is also extremely fast. Its top speed is 242 mph (389 kph). The doors open upward and look like a bat's wings.

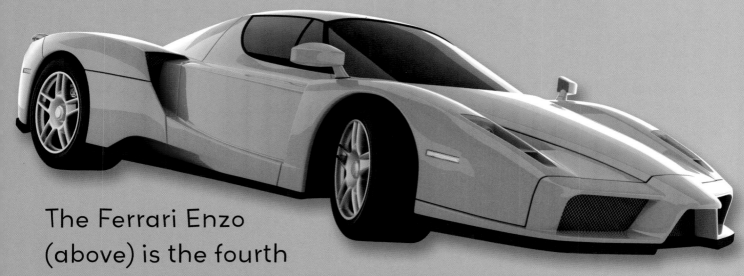

The Ferrari Enzo (above) is the fourth most expensive supercar. Ferrari is so proud of this supercar that they named it after their founder—Enzo Ferrari.

SUPERCARS IN THE MOVIES

Action movies often feature stars whizzing around in powerful supercars.

Tony Stark is the man inside the Iron Man suit. In the *Iron Man* films, he drives Audi R8 cars, like the one below.

Audi R8 5.2 FSI

The Audi R8 Spyder is handmade and has lots of amazing features. It can reach 62 mph (100 kph) in 4.1 seconds, and the spoiler slides out automatically when the car goes fast!

James Bond is an impressive supercar driver. In each film he has a brand new car and he always manages to crash it!

007's Supercars

Of course, James Bond doesn't have a normal supercar. His cars are built with weapons, ejector seats, and armor plating.

The latest films show James Bond driving an Aston Martin Vanquish or Aston Martin DBS.

FANTASY SUPERCARS

Some supercars are so amazing that they can only have come from a very creative imagination!

Batman's Batmobile is probably the coolest fantasy car there is. With rocket power and armor plating, Batman is sure to arrive safely.

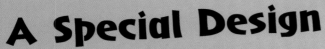

A Special Design

Director Steven Spielberg asked Lexus to use their latest technology to design a car (below) for the movie *Minority Report*. The car was custom built for the film's star Tom Cruise.

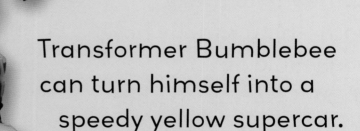

Transformer Bumblebee can turn himself into a speedy yellow supercar. In the movie, he becomes a Chevrolet Camaro supercar.

GLOSSARY

acceleration when a vehicle increases speed

aluminum a strong, light silver metal, which does not rust easily

armor plating very strong metal that is used to protect vehicles

carbon fiber a material that is very strong and very lightweight

commission to ask someone to make something exactly how you would like it

exhaust fumes the gas produced when an engine runs

features a part or quality of something

fuel gauge a device that tells you how much fuel is in the fuel tank

function the job that an object or gadget does

gadget a device with a clever design or unusual use

gull wing doors that have hinges at the top instead of the sides, so that they open upward

high-tech using the latest technology

hybrid a combination of two things

manufacturers people who make or build cars

pollute to make something unclean

prototype an experimental model that is made from the first designs

streamlined a smooth shape that air can pass over easily

unique one of a kind

FURTHER INFORMATION

Books

Awesome Supercars, (My Reading Library), Frances Ridley, New Forest Press, 2011.

Cars, (Machines on the Move), James Nixon, Amicus, 2011.

How Does a Car Work?, (How Does It Work?), Sarah Eason, Gareth Stevens Pub., 2010.

On the Road, (Machines Rule), Steve Parker, Smart Apple Media, 2010.

Record-Breaking Cars, (Record Breakers), Daniel Gilpin, Powerkids Press, 2012.

Websites

Find pictures and details of all the best supercars at Supercar World.
   www.supercarworld.com/cgi-bin/index.cgi

Search here for reviews and images of the top supercars.
   www.supercars.net/

The website for the TV series *Top Gear.*
   www.bbcamerica.com/shows/topgear/

INDEX